WISCONSIN

BY NATHAN SOMMER

BLASTOFF! DISCOVERY

BELLWETHER MEDIA • MINNEAPOLIS, MN

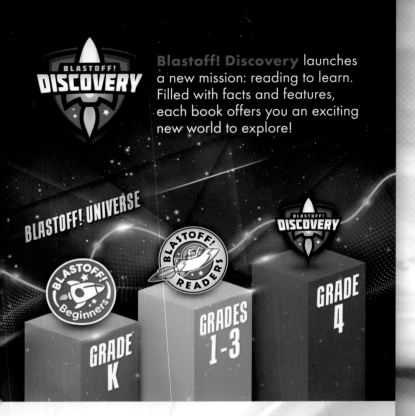

Blastoff! Discovery launches a new mission: reading to learn. Filled with facts and features, each book offers you an exciting new world to explore!

BLASTOFF! UNIVERSE

BLASTOFF! Beginners
GRADE K

BLASTOFF! READERS
GRADES 1-3

BLASTOFF! DISCOVERY
GRADE 4

This edition first published in 2022 by Bellwether Media, Inc.

No part of this publication may be reproduced in whole or in part without written permission of the publisher.
For information regarding permission, write to Bellwether Media, Inc.,
Attention: Permissions Department,
6012 Blue Circle Drive, Minnetonka, MN 55343.

Library of Congress Cataloging-in-Publication Data

Names: Sommer, Nathan, author.
Title: Wisconsin / by Nathan Sommer.
Description: Minneapolis, MN : Bellwether Media, Inc., 2022. |
   Series: Blastoff! Discovery: State profiles | Includes bibliographical
   references and index. | Audience: Ages 7-13 | Audience: Grades 4-6 |
   Summary: "Engaging images accompany information about Wisconsin.
   The combination of high-interest subject matter and narrative text is
   intended for students in grades 3 through 8"- Provided by publisher.
Identifiers: LCCN 2021020876 (print) | LCCN 2021020877 (ebook) |
   ISBN 9781644873564 (library binding) | ISBN 9781648341991 (ebook)
Subjects: LCSH: Wisconsin–Juvenile literature.
Classification: LCC F581.3 .S66 2022 (print) | LCC F581.3 (ebook) |
   DDC 977.5–dc23
LC record available at https://lccn.loc.gov/2021020876
LC ebook record available at https://lccn.loc.gov/2021020877

Editor: Colleen Sexton   Designer: Jeffrey Kollock

Printed in the United States of America, North Mankato, MN.

TABLE OF CONTENTS

A family is exploring the Wisconsin Dells in a Duck.
These unusual boats drive on land and travel through water!
The Duck heads down a wooded trail where the family spies
a deer. Splash! The Duck lands in the Wisconsin River.
The family cruises between **canyon** walls. Amazing formations
look like piled up slabs of rock. A melting **glacier** carved
them about 15,000 years ago.

GREAT ROCKS

The rock in the Wisconsin Dells is sandstone. It has been around for more than 500 million years. The tallest structures are more than 100 feet (30 meters) high!

OTHER TOP SITES

APOSTLE ISLANDS

DEVIL'S LAKE STATE PARK

MILWAUKEE ART MUSEUM

THREE EAGLE TRAIL

The Duck arrives at the Sugar Bowl, a giant rounded island. This type of formation exists in only a few places around the world. Soon the Duck rolls out of the water. What an adventure!

Wisconsin is in the **Upper Midwest** region of the United States. Michigan's Upper **Peninsula** and Lake Superior border northern Wisconsin. There, the 21 Apostle Islands form a chain along the shoreline. Minnesota and Iowa are Wisconsin's western neighbors. The Mississippi River forms part of the state's western border. Illinois lies south of Wisconsin. Lake Michigan washes its eastern border. The lake cuts into the northeastern shoreline to create Green Bay.

Wisconsin covers 65,496 square miles (169,634 square kilometers). The capital, Madison, sits in southern Wisconsin. Other major cities include Milwaukee, Green Bay, and Racine.

MINNESOTA

IOWA

LAKE SUPERIOR

APOSTLE ISLANDS

UPPER PENINSULA
MICHIGAN

WISCONSIN
RIVER

GREEN BAY

GREEN BAY

WISCONSIN

APPLETON

LAKE
MICHIGAN

MADISON

MILWAUKEE

N
W — E
S

MISSISSIPPI
RIVER

RACINE

KENOSHA

ILLINOIS

ALL IN A NAME

Wisconsin comes from an Algonquin word meaning "river running through a red place." The Miami people gave this name to the Wisconsin River. It flows through the middle of the state.

7

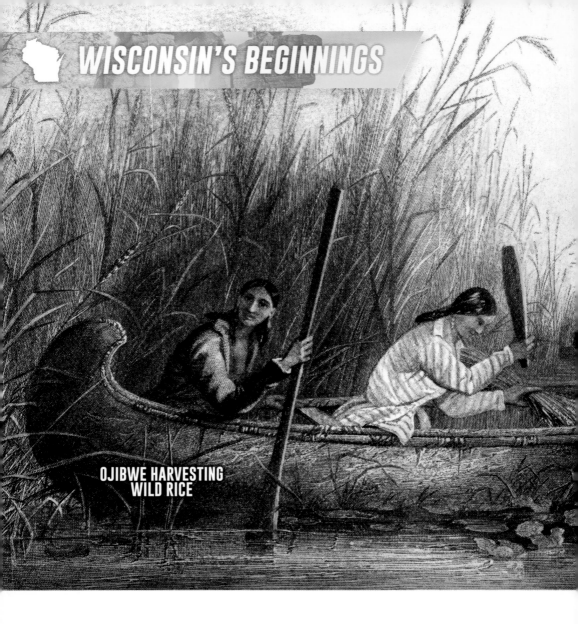

OJIBWE HARVESTING
WILD RICE

People first arrived in Wisconsin around 10,000 years ago. They formed Native American tribes over time. The Ho-Chunk, Menominee, and Ojibwe were some of the largest groups. These hunters and farmers lived in villages. In 1634, French explorer Jean Nicolet landed at Green Bay. French fur traders and **missionaries** soon followed.

The British gained Wisconsin from France in 1763 after the **French and Indian War**. The United States took control after the **Revolutionary War**. In the 1820s, people started pouring into Wisconsin to mine lead. The population boomed. Wisconsin became the 30th state in 1848.

THE ORIGINAL BADGERS

In the 1820s, miners in Wisconsin dug makeshift homes out of rock in their mines. They became known as "badger boys." That is how Wisconsin earned the nickname the Badger State.

NATIVE PEOPLES OF WISCONSIN

ONEIDA NATION OF WISCONSIN

- Original lands in New York, then northern Wisconsin
- Around 16,500 in Wisconsin today

MENOMINEE INDIAN TRIBE OF WISCONSIN

- Original lands near the Great Lakes in Wisconsin, Michigan, and Illinois
- More than 8,700 in Wisconsin today

CHIPPEWA

- Original lands in northern Wisconsin
- Six federally recognized tribes in Wisconsin
- More than 25,000 in Wisconsin today
- Also called Ojibwe and Anishinaabe

HO-CHUNK NATION

- Original lands in eastern Wisconsin
- More than 7,800 in Wisconsin today
- Once known as the Wisconsin Winnebago Tribe

The Superior Upland region covers the northern half of Wisconsin. Thick pine forests spread across rolling hills. The state's tallest point, Timm's Hill, rises there. Thousands of lakes dot the region. The land slopes down to the Central **Plains** of southern Wisconsin. Rivers flow through grassy **prairies** and farmland. Eastern Wisconsin is home to Lake Winnebago, the state's largest lake. Rocky cliffs overlook the Mississippi River in the southwest.

TIMM'S HILL

LAKE WINNEBAGO—

—MISSISSIPPI RIVER

SUPERIOR UPLAND
CENTRAL PLAINS

N
W—+—E
S

LAKE WINNEBAGO IN WINTER

SPRING
HIGH: 56°F (13°C)
LOW: 36°F (2°C)

SUMMER
HIGH: 80°F (27°C)
LOW: 59°F (15°C)

FALL
HIGH: 59°F (15°C)
LOW: 40°F (4°C)

WINTER
HIGH: 29°F (-2°C)
LOW: 13°F (-11°C)

°F = degrees Fahrenheit
°C = degrees Celsius

WISCONSIN'S CHALLENGE: CLIMATE CHANGE AND FLOODING

Climate change is making Wisconsin warmer and wetter. More rain along with quickly melting snow puts the state in danger of spring flooding. Floods can damage buildings, destroy crops, and spill chemicals into the water supply.

Wisconsin has long, cold winters and short, muggy summers. It is at risk for winter blizzards and spring floods. Tornadoes often strike during the summer months.

Black bears roam Wisconsin's thick forests. There, porcupines, raccoons, and white-tailed deer watch out for coyotes, wolves, and other predators. Otters and beavers share the state's many rivers with trout, bass, and walleye. Great gray owls, red-tailed hawks, and other birds of prey swoop down from above to grab dinner. Painted turtles, bullfrogs, and garter snakes live near wetlands.

Foxes, skunks, and badgers find shelter in Wisconsin's prairies. Pheasants and wild turkeys peck the ground for seeds and insects. The state is also an important stop for **migrating** Canada geese and sandhill cranes.

COYOTE

WALLEYE

GARTER SNAKE

NORTH AMERICAN PORCUPINE

SANDHILL CRANES

A TURKEY COMEBACK

Wisconsin had almost no wild turkeys during the 1970s. Today, with about 350,000 wild turkeys, the state has one of the country's largest populations!

AMERICAN BADGER

Life Span: up to 14 years
Status: least concern

American badger range =

LEAST CONCERN	NEAR THREATENED	VULNERABLE	ENDANGERED	CRITICALLY ENDANGERED	EXTINCT IN THE WILD	EXTINCT

13

PEOPLE AND COMMUNITIES

More than 5.8 million people call Wisconsin home. Two of every three live in cities. The Milwaukee area alone has about 1.5 million residents. Central and western Wisconsin are more **rural**.

MADISON

FAMOUS WISCONSINITE

Name: Mark Ruffalo
Born: November 22, 1967
Hometown: Kenosha, Wisconsin
Famous For: Actor and Academy Award nominee who is best known for playing the Hulk in *The Avengers* and other Marvel Cinematic Universe movies

Wisconsinites come from many backgrounds. Around 9 of every 10 have **ancestors** from Europe, including Germany, Ireland, and Poland. Smaller numbers of Black or African Americans live in Wisconsin. The state has 11 federally recognized Native American tribes. A growing number of Hispanics call southeastern Wisconsin home. Newcomers have arrived from Mexico, India, and China.

PRAIRIE STYLE

Frank Lloyd Wright was a famous architect from Wisconsin. He developed the Prairie style of architecture. Wisconsin's bluffs and valleys inspired the buildings he created in this style.

In 1846, three villages joined together to found Milwaukee on Lake Michigan. The city quickly became a major grain port. Today, Milwaukee stretches along Lake Michigan. It is Wisconsin's largest and most **diverse** city. Together, Black or African Americans and Hispanics make up three of every five residents.

LAKE EMILY

Downtown Milwaukee has an underground lake. Lake Emily was a popular fishing and swimming spot before an office was built on top of it in 1905.

MITCHELL PARK HORTICULTURAL CONSERVATORY

Locals can get around downtown on the Hop streetcar system. The Milwaukee RiverWalk connects the city's restaurants, parks, and offices along the Milwaukee River. Sailors and kite-flyers head to Lake Michigan's shore. The Milwaukee Art Museum showcases art from around the world. Visitors stroll through the dome-covered gardens of the Mitchell Park Horticultural Conservatory.

CRANBERRY BOG
MANITOWISH WATERS

Wisconsin is known as America's Dairyland. The state is a national leader in milk and cheese production. Farmers raise more than 1.2 million dairy cows! Other major crops include corn, wheat, soybeans, and cranberries. Wisconsin's cranberry bogs produce more than any other state.

WISCONSIN'S CHALLENGE: A WORKER SHORTAGE

Companies across Wisconsin are struggling to find young employees to replace retiring workers. More people are leaving the state after college to find work. This hurts Wisconsin's economy and its ability to develop new products and services.

Manufacturing is another major industry. Wisconsin's factory workers make machinery, metal products, paper, and chemicals. Most residents have service jobs. Many work in hospitals, banks, and schools. Campgrounds, theme parks, and other tourist spots also employ many service workers.

INVENTED IN WISCONSIN

QWERTY KEYBOARD
Date Invented: 1873
Inventor: Christopher Latham Sholes

MALTED MILK
Date Invented: 1873
Inventors: William and James Horlick

BLENDER
Date Invented: 1922
Inventor: Stephen Poplawski

AMERICAN GIRL DOLL
Date Invented: 1986
Inventor: Pleasant Rowland

BRATWURSTS

Wisconsinites make meals inspired by their European backgrounds. They grill or boil German bratwursts at cookouts. Swedish pancakes are another favorite. Wisconsinites often top these big folded breakfast treats with lingonberries. Wisconsin is famous for Danish kringles. Bakers sometimes fill these oval-shaped pastries with cranberries grown in the state.

THE CHEESIEST STATE

Wisconsin has around 7,000 dairy farms. Some of the milk they produce is turned into about 3.4 billion pounds (1.5 billion kilograms) of cheese each year. That is about one-fourth of the country's cheese!

Wisconsinites also celebrate their state's dairy products. Menus across the state feature beer cheese soup topped with popcorn. Plain or fried cheese curds make a great snack. Brave eaters try the stinky limburger cheese sandwich with mustard and onions.

BEER CHEESE SOUP

FRIED CHEESE CURDS

DANISH KRINGLE

12 SERVINGS

Have an adult help you make this sweet treat! This kringle will be rectangle-shaped.

INGREDIENTS

1 premade refrigerated piecrust, softened as directed on the box

2/3 cup chopped pecans

1/3 cup packed brown sugar

3 tablespoons butter, softened

white icing

water

DIRECTIONS

1. Heat the oven to 375 degrees Fahrenheit (191 degrees Celsius). Place the uncovered piecrust flat on a large, ungreased cookie sheet.

2. In a medium bowl, mix pecans, brown sugar, and butter. Sprinkle the mixture over half of the piecrust to within 3/4 inch of the edge.

3. Brush the edge with water. Fold the piecrust over the filling. Move the kringle to the center of the cookie sheet. Press the edge with a fork to seal it. Then poke the top with a fork.

4. Bake for 17 to 22 minutes or until golden brown. Cool for 5 minutes. Drizzle white icing on top.

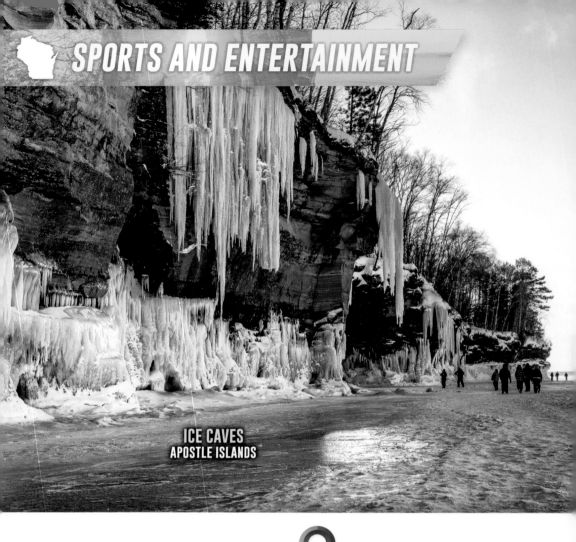

ICE CAVES
APOSTLE ISLANDS

Wisconsin has thousands of lakes. Locals explore them by kayak, ferry, and sailboat. On land, residents tour historic lighthouses. They hike shorelines statewide. During winter, snowmobilers zoom along forested trails. Ice caves on the Apostle Islands draw winter hikers.

THE BIRKIE

The American Birkebeiner, or the Birkie, is the largest cross-country ski race in the United States. More than 10,000 skiers head to Hayward each February for this event.

Football is big in Wisconsin. Green Bay Packer fans are known for wearing cheese-shaped hats. Wisconsinites also cheer for the Milwaukee Bucks basketball team and the Milwaukee Brewers baseball team. Art fans check out works from around the world at Madison's Chazen Museum of Art. Others head to Spring Green to tour the Taliesin home designed by Frank Lloyd Wright.

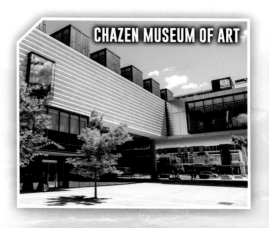

CHAZEN MUSEUM OF ART

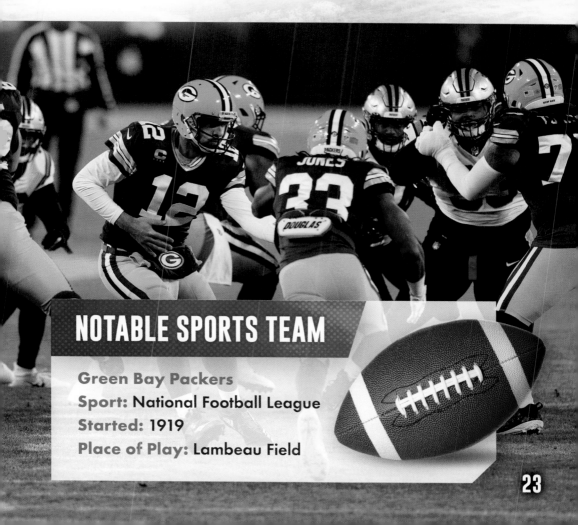

NOTABLE SPORTS TEAM

Green Bay Packers
Sport: National Football League
Started: 1919
Place of Play: Lambeau Field

Milwaukee's Summerfest is one of the world's largest music festivals. More than 700,000 people watch top artists perform each July. Green County Cheese Days is the Midwest's oldest food festival. Guests have enjoyed its cow-milking contests and dairy farm tours since 1914. La Crosse hosts one of the country's largest Oktoberfest celebrations. It features a parade and **traditional** German costumes, songs, and food.

SUMMERFEST

HONOR THE EARTH POWWOW
HAYWARD

The Honor the Earth **Powwow** is in Hayward.
It showcases traditional Native American music, dances,
and food. A carnival, parade, and cranberry treats
bring crowds to the Cranberry Blossom Festival in
Wisconsin Rapids. Wisconsinites have a lot to celebrate!

1836
Madison is named the capital of the Wisconsin Territory

1634
French explorer Jean Nicolet lands near Green Bay on the shores of Lake Michigan

1783
The United States wins the Revolutionary War and takes control of Wisconsin

1763
Great Britain wins the French and Indian War and gains control of Wisconsin

1822
Lead miners begin moving into Wisconsin

1960

Dena Smith becomes the first woman elected to a statewide office in Wisconsin

1861-1865

Wisconsin soldiers fight for the Union in the Civil War

1919

Wisconsin is the first state to approve the Nineteenth Amendment, giving women the right to vote

1848

Wisconsin becomes the 30th state

2011

The Green Bay Packers win their fourth Super Bowl

Nicknames: The Badger State, America's Dairyland

Motto: Forward

Date of Statehood: May 29, 1848 (the 30th state)

Capital City: Madison ★

Other Major Cities: Milwaukee, Green Bay, Kenosha, Racine, Appleton

Area: 65,496 square miles (169,634 square kilometers); Wisconsin is the 23rd largest state.

Population

5,893,718
(2020)

STATE FLAG

Wisconsin's flag was adopted in 1913. It displays the state name and date of statehood on a blue background. The state coat of arms sits in the center. It features a sailor and a miner holding a shield. The shield has symbols for farming, mining, navigation, and manufacturing. The state animal, the badger, sits on top of the shield. A banner above has the state motto.

INDUSTRY

Main Exports

medical equipment

machinery

aircraft

processed foods

computers

chemicals

JOBS

- MANUFACTURING **13%**
- FARMING AND NATURAL RESOURCES **3%**
- GOVERNMENT **12%**
- SERVICES **72%**

Natural Resources
sand, cement, limestone, coal

GOVERNMENT

Federal Government

8 REPRESENTATIVES | **2** SENATORS

WI

10 ELECTORAL VOTES

USA

State Government

99 REPRESENTATIVES | **33** SENATORS

STATE SYMBOLS

STATE BIRD
AMERICAN ROBIN

STATE ANIMAL
AMERICAN BADGER

STATE FLOWER
WOOD VIOLET

STATE TREE
SUGAR MAPLE

GLOSSARY

ancestors—relatives who lived long ago

canyon—a deep and narrow valley that has steep sides

diverse—made up of people or things that are different from one another

French and Indian War—a war between Great Britain and France over land in North America that was part of a larger war between Great Britain and France called the Seven Years' War

glacier—a massive sheet of ice that covers a large area of land

manufacturing—a field of work in which people use machines to make products

migrating—traveling from one place to another, often with the seasons

missionaries—people sent to a place to spread a religious faith

peninsula—a section of land that extends out from a larger piece of land and is almost completely surrounded by water

plains—large areas of flat land

powwow—a Native American gathering that usually includes dancing

prairies—large, open areas of grassland

Revolutionary War—the war from 1775 to 1783 in which the United States fought for independence from Great Britain

rural—related to the countryside

service jobs—jobs that perform tasks for people or businesses

tourist—related to the business of people traveling to visit other places

traditional—related to customs, ideas, or beliefs handed down from one generation to the next

Upper Midwest—a region of the United States that includes Minnesota, Wisconsin, Michigan, Iowa, North Dakota, and South Dakota

AT THE LIBRARY

Bekkering, Annalise. *Great Lakes*. New York, N.Y.: AV2 by Weigl, 2020.

Hunter, Tony. *Green Bay Packers*. Minneapolis, Minn.: Abdo Publishing, 2020.

Micklos, John, Jr., Richard Hantula, and Margaret Dornfeld. *Wisconsin*. New York, N.Y.: Cavendish Square, 2019.

ON THE WEB

FACTSURFER

Factsurfer.com gives you a safe, fun way to find more information.

1. Go to www.factsurfer.com.

2. Enter "Wisconsin" into the search box and click 🔍.

3. Select your book cover to see a list of related content.

INDEX